BIBLICAL STORIES FROM A-Z

By Tarsha Phillips

Copyright © 2021 Tarsha Phillips

Copyright © 2021 Lady Knight Enterprises Publishing

Duluth, Georgia

www.ladyknightenterprisespublishing.com

All rights reserved. No part of this publication, contents and/or cover may be reproduced in whole or in part in any form without the express, written permission of the Author or Publisher. This includes stored in a retrieval system, or transmitted in any form or means, for example but not limited to; photocopying, recording, electronic copying, mechanical, scanning, or otherwise. It is illegal to copy this book, post it to a website, or distribute it by any other means without written permission from the Author or Publisher.

Printed in the United States of America.

BIBLICAL STORIES FROM A-Z

ISBN-13: 978-1-7358663-2-1

(Lady Knight Enterprises Publishing)

Cover artwork created by George Robinson

Sign Language provided by Tarsha Phillips

DEDICATION

This book is dedicated to ALL God's children!

CONTENTS

	Acknowledgments	i
1	ABRAHAM	1
2	BENJAMIN	3
3	CHRIST	5
4	DAVID	8
5	ELIZABETH	10
6	FAITH	12
7	GABRIEL	13
8	HANNAH	14
9	ISRAEL	16
10	JESSE	17
11	KING	18
12	LUKE	19
13	MOSES	20

14	NOAH	22
15	ORPAH	23
16	PAUL	24
17	QUARTUS & RUTH	25
18	SOLOMON	27
19	TIMOTHY	29
20	UZZIAH	30
21	VICTORY	31
22	WORLD	32
23	XERXES	33
24	YAHWEH	35
25	ZADOK	36

ACKNOWLDGMENTS

I would like to acknowledge God first, then my children and my family, for all their support they have shown, in all my endeavors!

CHAPTER 1

ABRAHAM

Abraham was married to Sarah. They did not think they could have any children, which was a disappointment, because they really wanted a family. But, God had a greater plan for Abraham (Genesis 2l).

When Abraham was 75 years old, God made a promise to him that he would have lots of children. God even promised that the Savior would come through Abraham's family. All God asked, was that Abraham and Sarah leave their home and follow Him. They had a hard choice to make; leave all their friends and follow God or stay comfortable. Would you leave all of your friends and follow God? This was not easy.

Abraham wanted children, but was already a bit old. Sarah wasn't so young herself. So if Abraham and Sarah were going to leave their home, they had to trust and believe that God was going to do something impossible. They decided to trust that God would keep His promise. This is always the right choice!

Abraham and Sarah traveled from their home to a land called Canaan. Right away, God reminded Abraham of His promise. God said, "I will multiply your children, as many as the granules of sands on the seashore." This was God's way of telling Abraham that he would have a lot of children.

After a while, Abraham and Sarah still had no children together. God took Abraham out one night and told him to look at the stars. He reminded Abraham that He would give him that many children. Abraham decided to keep believing God. He and Sarah waited.

After many, many years passed, Abraham and Sarah grew tired of waiting. This time God told Abraham, the next year Sarah would have a son. Abraham was 99 years old! He and Sarah had both given up on God's promise to have children. When Sarah overheard the message from God, she laughed! Sarah was tired of waiting and had lost all hope. The great thing is, even when we think it is impossible, God does keep His promises. And just as God had promised, Sarah was with child the next year. Isaac was born when Abraham was 100 years old, and Sarah was 89. Isaac means 'laughter.'

Even though it seemed impossible, it was easy for God, because He can do anything. And remember how God was going to give Abraham as many children as the stars in the sky? Well, Isaac grew up and had children, who had more children, who had more children. This kept going and going and going. And yes, the Savior Himself, was eventually born in Abraham's line. All because Abraham and Sarah obeyed God and trusted God to keep His promise.

Where is this story found in the Bible: Genesis 21

Can GOD do something that seems impossible?

Is there anything too difficult for GOD to handle?

A B R A H A M

CHAPTER 2

BENJAMIN

Benjamin was the twelfth and youngest son of Jacob. His mother was Rachel, Jacob's wife. Benjamin was born during the journey that Jacob and his family took from Padan Aram, to Canaan.

His mother Rachel was about to die, but with her last breath, she named the baby Ben-oni, meaning 'Son of my sorrow.' The baby's father, called him Benjamin, which means, 'son of my right hand.'

Joseph, Benjamin's brother, was sold into slavery by his other brothers. Later, Joseph became prime minister of Egypt.

A famine spread across the land. One day, Jacob (now called Israel), and his sons ran out of food. Israel told them to go back to Egypt and purchase more food. Judah, Israel's son, insisted that they take Benjamin with them. Joseph had told them that they could not buy more food unless they brought Benjamin with them.

Israel did not want to send Benjamin with them, because he was afraid of losing Benjamin. Then Judah said that he would guarantee Benjamin's safe return. Israel trusted God and sent Benjamin to Egypt with his brothers. He also sent a present, and extra money to Joseph. Would you like to know what was included in the present Israel sent to the Prime Minister? **Genesis 43:11,** *"Then their father Israel said to them, "If it must be, then do this: Put some of the best products of the land in your bags and take them down to the man as a gift-a little balm and a little honey, some spices and myrrh, some pistachio nuts and almonds."*

When they arrived in Egypt, Joseph saw Benjamin and ordered his steward to take them to his house, and to get ready for a feast. The steward gave them water to wash their feet and fed their donkeys.

Joseph asked about their father, and blessed Benjamin. Then he went to his room and cried. When he returned, his servants served the food. The brothers were seated according to their ages. Joseph gave Benjamin five times as much food, than to his other brothers.

Later, Joseph's brothers refused to abandon Benjamin. After Joseph put them to a test, he realized his brothers had a change of heart, and were willing to risk their lives for their youngest brother. Through this test, the whole family of Jacob was reunited.

In Genesis 49:27, Jacob blesses his 12 sons, he describes Benjamin as a wolf, a hunter who hunted all morning and evening, after his prey. He would divide the prey in the evening.

<u>Where is this story found in the Bible: Genesis 49</u>

Your name helps develop your identity. Why do you think Jacob changed the baby's name?

What does your name mean?

CHAPTER 3

CHRIST

Jesus Christ, the Messiah-Savior, and the Son of God. He came to earth to show people how to follow God and how to love and care for others. Jesus was born in Bethlehem. Mary was His mother.

Shepherds were tending their sheep nearby, when an angel appeared to them, announcing the coming of the Messiah-Savior. A bright star appeared in the sky, and the shepherds followed it to the town of Bethlehem, to worship Baby Jesus Christ. Yes, a bright star appeared in the sky. Just like the angel said, and they found baby Jesus Christ with His parents, wrapped in swaddling clothes and lying in a manager. They bowed down and worshipped the Savior of the world.

Do you know what swaddling clothes are? Swaddling clothes were strips of cloth, probably cotton, not really clothes. The custom was to wrap the baby in these strips of cloth after washing and anointing the baby.

Now, do you know what a manger is? Well, a manger is not a baby crib. Baby Jesus Christ was laid in a long open wooden box, used for horses or cattle to eat from. For baby Jesus, they filled it with hay.

Jesus grew up and began to perform countless miracles. Would you like to hear about a few of these amazing miracles?

- Who was Jesus Christ - There were large crowds that gathered around Jesus all throughout His ministry. He healed some of them, from life threatening diseases. He fed over 5,000 people, with just 5 loaves of bread and 2 fish. He also raised some who were dead, back to life.

- Jesus Christ calmed the storm - Jesus Christ and the disciples were crossing the sea of Galilee, in a boat one evening, when a terrible storm appeared. The ship was filled with water and the disciples were afraid. Jesus Christ was asleep, but they woke Him up. When Jesus Christ woke up, He spoke to the wind and to the waves to be calm. Immediately the wind and waves calmed down. (Mark 4:35-40)

- Jesus Christ walks on water - Jesus Christ sent His disciples across the sea of Galilee one night, while He went to the mountains to pray. The disciples obeyed and went to their boat. But during the night there was a storm. The storm pushed the boat out to sea. The disciples worked hard to get the boat to land, although their efforts failed. Early in the morning, they saw a man walking on the water! They were afraid. They did not know it was Jesus coming to be with them. Jesus Christ called out to the disciples in the boat and told them not to be afraid. Jesus Christ told them who He was. As Jesus Christ came to them, the storm began to calm. (Matthew 14:22-33)

- Jesus Christ heals a blind man - Jesus Christ's disciples were surprised each and every time, He did a miracle. While in the city of Bethsaida, the people asked Jesus to touch the man, so that he could see again. They knew Jesus had power to heal people. Jesus took the blind man and led him out of the city. He healed the man by spitting on his eyes and touching them. Jesus asked the man if he could see anything. The man opened his eyes and said that he could see men, walking around like trees. Jesus then put His hands on the man's eyes again. After this, the man could see clearly. (Mark 8:22-26)

Did you know that Jesus Christ blesses children? This story is found in the scriptures of Matthew 19:13-15; Mark 10:13-16; and Luke 18:15-17. Jesus Christ and His disciples had left a place called Capernaum, and crossed into Judea. This was Jesus Christ's final journey toward Jerusalem. In a village, people began bringing their little children to Jesus Christ, to have Him bless them. The disciple's told the people not to bother Jesus.

Jesus Christ told His followers: "Let the little children come to me, and do not hinder them, for the kingdom of God belongs to such as these. I tell you the truth, anyone who will not receive the kingdom of God like a little child, will never enter it." (Luke 18:16-17)

Jesus Christ blesses us every moment, with blessings which we can see, and some which we cannot see. He is able to still do many wonderful miracles. Each of these miracles helps us understand that Jesus Christ is God's Son, and that He has control over all things!

BIBLICAL STORIES FROM A-Z

Where is this story found in the Bible: The Books of Matthew, Mark, & Luke

What was the greatest act of Jesus for all people in the world?

Did Jesus care about children? What did HE say about them?

C H R I S T

CHAPTER 4

DAVID

David was Jesse's youngest son and God's chosen king of Israel, after King Saul. God was disappointed in Saul, the king of Israel. He told the prophet Samuel to anoint another person as king. The Lord said to the prophet, "Fill your horn with oil. Go to Bethlehem, where you will find a man named Jesse. I have provided for myself a king, from among his sons." Samuel traveled to Bethlehem and arrived at the home of Jesse, where he was to have a blessing ceremony. Jesse and his boys joined Samuel, as requested.

Eliab was the first son to come forth. Samuel saw the young man and thought to himself, "Surely this is the one the Lord wants me to anoint as king." But the Lord said to Samuel, "Do not look on his appearance, or on his height, because I have rejected him; for the Lord does not see as humans see. Humans look on the outward appearance, but the Lord looks on the heart."

Jesse called another son up, to bring before Samuel, but the Lord said to him, "Neither has the Lord chosen this one." Jesse brought seven of his sons before Samuel, but the Lord said that none of them were his chosen one. Finally, Samuel said to Jesse, "Are all your sons here?" Jesse said, "No, there is one more, my youngest son, David. He is out in the fields, keeping the sheep." "Send for him and bring him to me," the prophet said. Jesse sent for David, who arrived soon afterward. The Lord spoke suddenly to Samuel saying, "Rise, and anoint him; for this is the one." The prophet, Samuel, took the horn of olive oil and anointed the youngest son, in the presence of all of his older brothers. The spirit of the Lord came powerfully upon David, from that day on.

While still yet a young boy, David fearlessly killed a 9 foot giant, by the name of Goliath, with only a sling and a stone. King Saul liked David in the beginning, however because of David's growing popularity, King Saul became very jealous of David. The Israelite's had to fight a war with the Philistines, in which the Israelites lost. King Saul lost his three sons in battle. King Saul did not want to be tortured and put to death by the Philistine army. His armor bearer knew that he was not to kill the Lord's anointed and was too fearful to take King Saul's life. The Bible says King Saul fell upon his own sword, and he died. (1 Samuel 31:4-6)

After Saul died, there was no danger for David. David returned to his own land. His own tribe of Judah made him the king, just as the Prophet Samuel had said when David was a little boy. Time passed, the rest of Saul's son's also died. David was then made the king of the entire kingdom of Israel. David was thirty years old when he became king, and he reigned forty years (2 Samuel 5:4). When the Philistines heard this, they decided to attack. But David proved to be a brave, clever and strong king. He defeated the Philistine army and sent them running for the hills. David decided to take Jerusalem, as his capital city. The Jebusite's tried to do everything possible to stop David from entering their city. David found underground tunnels leading to the city, so he sent soldiers inside the city to open the gates. David took Jerusalem by surprise, making it his capital city.

The life of King David, ends after his son Solomon, by his wife Bathsheba, was named the next ruler of Israel. King David died at the age of seventy.

Where is this story found in the Bible: 1 Samuel 31; 2 Samuel 5

Why did GOD have to choose a new king for Israel?

Who did the Lord tell Samuel to anoint?

CHAPTER 5

ELIZABETH

Elizabeth and her husband, Zechariah, both came from a long line of priests. They both loved God and obeyed His commandments; they were righteous in God's eyes. They really wanted a family, but Elizabeth could not have children.

As they grew older and older, their dream of having a child seemed impossible. One day when Zechariah and the group of priests, were serving at the Temple, he was chosen to burn incense in the Temple. Suddenly, an Angel of the Lord appeared next to the altar of incense. Yes, right before Zechariah! Zechariah was afraid, but the Angel told him not to be afraid. The Angel then gave Zechariah wonderful news! Your prayers have been heard! Elizabeth will give you a son, and you will name him John. Zechariah wanted to believe the Angel, but he and his wife were so old. Zechariah asked the Angel, "How can this be true?" In a thundering voice, the Angel replied, "I am Gabriel, I stand before God Himself. The Lord has sent me to give you this good news." The Angel Gabriel told Zechariah, that because of his unbelief, he would not be able to speak until after the child was born. Zechariah left the Temple, and went home, unable to tell anyone of his meeting with the Angel.

Later, just as the Angel said, Elizabeth was bearing a child (that means having a baby inside of her). During the 6th month of Elizabeth's childbearing, God sent the Angel to visit one of Elizabeth's cousin, a young woman named Mary. Mary was about to be married. Gabriel told Mary that she had found favor with the Lord. She would give birth to King Jesus. He would be King of Kings, and Lord of Lords.

Mary would give birth to the Messiah. Mary quickly ran to visit her cousin Elizabeth, who lived in Judea. When Mary arrived and spoke to Elizabeth, Elizabeth's baby leaped inside of her. Elizabeth blessed Mary.

BIBLICAL STORIES FROM A-Z

Later, Elizabeth gave birth to a healthy son. Friends and family came to visit. They were thinking that their baby would be named Zechariah, after his father. But Zechariah, still unable to speak, wrote on a stone tablet the name "John." Suddenly, Zechariah could speak again! Their son would be known as John the Baptist, and he would prepare generations for the coming of Jesus the Messiah!

Where is this story found in the Bible: Luke 1

Even if it takes a long time, does GOD always keep HIS promise?

What type of person do you need to be, even when waiting on GOD to answer your prayers?

ELIZABETH

CHAPTER 6

FAITH

Faith is mentioned in the King James Version of the Bible, 231 times. The Bible tells us that without faith, it is impossible to please God. (Hebrews 11:6) Faith is believing in something you can't necessarily prove. Faith is a gift from God. God loves us and He can do all things. This means God is always able to take care of us. We can trust God. When we go through our day trusting God and knowing He will help take care of us, that is living in faith. When we live in faith we are blessed. When we trust God, we find out that He keeps His word. This helps us trust Him even more, the next time.

Still confused? Faith is like a house; it must be built on a very strong foundation if it is going to stand against the storms and the rains. Let's use the Word of God. Faith's foundation is the Word of God. You cannot build a solid faith life without it. The best part about this truth is that the Word of God will never fail. God wants to be the foundation of your personal house of faith, meaning your body. You can trust Him to do what He says. It is absolutely necessary we know God's promises so that we can begin to build our houses (bodies) of faith, for "faith cometh by hearing, and hearing by the word of God," (Roman 10:17). It is only as we hear God's Word, His promises concerning us, that our faith will grow, and be solid as a rock. The Bible is God's Word, therefore make a choice to believe in all that He says. God is still fulfilling His promises today.

Where is this story found in the Bible: Hebrews 11:6; Romans 10:17

Who do you have Faith in?

How can your Faith in God grow more?

CHAPTER 7

GABRIEL

Gabriel - We know from scripture, the angel Gabriel is a messenger, who God trusted to deliver several important messages. Gabriel means 'God is great,' and as the messenger, he is the one who revealed that the Savior would be called "Jesus."

Gabriel appeared to three people in the Bible. He first appeared to Daniel, after the prophet had a vision. Gabriel's role was to explain the vision to Daniel.

God sent the angel Gabriel, to deliver a special message to Mary. Gabriel told Mary she would be the mother of the Son of God. Mary did not believe how she could have a miracle baby, Jesus! She was honored to be God's servant.

Also, the angel Gabriel, was sent to Zechariah, to tell of the news that Elizabeth would have a son.

Gabriel is an archangel. Archangels are God's high-ranking angels, that do special assignments. These are great examples about angels, and how they are sent to give messages from God.

Where are these stories found in the Bible: Daniel 8 & 9; Luke 1

What is one main task given to angels?

What is an archangel?

CHAPTER 8

HANNAH

Hannah, whose name means 'gracious gift or compassion,' was a woman in the Bible who showed self-discipline, perseverance, and faith. Her greatest desire was to be a mother, but GOD had not answered her prayer. Because of this, she was in deep sorrow and sadness. Now, she was one of the wives of Elkanah, who loved her very much, but for years Peninnah, Elkanah's other wife, bullied and taunted Hannah, because she did not have any children. In that time period, men were allowed to have more than one wife. Hannah had such self-discipline, she never tried to get revenge, or argue back with Peninnah, but kept silent, expecting God to one day bless her, with a child.

Their tradition at that time, was to go to the temple once a year to worship and offer sacrifices to God. While there, the priest (pastor) would give the husband the sacrificial meal to eat, and he would give food to his family. This is similar to the 'Communion,' with bread and wine, that we take at church, today. Elkanah would eat, and give some of the food to Peninnah, and her children. Then he would give a larger portion to Hannah, because he loved her very much, and he felt bad for her not being able to have children.

Once again, at the temple, Peninnah began to bully Hannah, and laugh at her, because she didn't have children. Hannah became so upset, she refused to eat and began to cry. Elkanah began to console her, and for him, she ate a little.

This trip to the temple was unlike the others, because soon after eating, Hannah slipped away from the table, and went to the sanctuary to pray. The priest (pastor), who was watching as people were praying, was named Eli.

Hannah's heart was already broken into pieces, because she didn't have children, and being bullied by Peninnah, just made matters worse. Hannah began to sob and pray. She made a vow with God that if He gave her a son, she would bring him back to the temple, and dedicate him to the priesthood, as God's servant.

Well like many of us, Hannah wasn't praying out loud, but silently, in her heart. Tears continued to run down her face, and her lips were moving, but no sound came out. Eli, the priest, was watching closely, and thought she was acting strangely. He couldn't hear her, but could see her lips move, and accused her of being drunk, in front of everyone. However, Hannah stood, and with respect, told Eli she was not drunk, but brokenhearted, and was just pouring out her heart to God.

Later that year, God did answer Hannah's prayer, and blessed her with a son, Samuel. When the child was big enough to help with chores, she kept her word to God, took Samuel to the temple, and dedicated him to be trained up, as a priest. After his dedication, Elkanah and Hannah worshipped God, before leaving the temple.

<u>Where is this story found in the Bible: 1 Samuel</u>

Do you think Hannah was a faithful believer in God?

Why?

CHAPTER 9

ISRAEL

Israel means 'God's people,' and the people who are identified with this name, are chosen by God, as the people who His Son Jesus, would be born to. They would be the first people to have the opportunity to believe in Jesus. They were considered a holy people; God's people. The name Israel, was also given to who was Abraham's grandson, after he, Jacob wrestled with an angel. From Jacob's twelve sons, the twelve tribes of Israel were born, and became the nation of Israel.

This is the same nation of people that became slaves in Egypt, and God sent Moses to tell Pharoah, to let His people go. This is the same nation of people that stayed in the wilderness for 40 years, because of their unbelief.

This is the same nation of people GOD prepared to live in Canaan, the 'Promised Land,' just as He had promised to Abraham, hundreds of years earlier.

This is the same nation of people, where the virgin Mary, gave birth to baby Jesus, in the little town of Bethlehem. This is the same nation of people, who had Jesus crucified, on a cross.

Where is this story found in the Bible: Genesis 32

What name was given to the first people who had an opportunity to believe in Jesus?

Name something you learned about this nation of people.

CHAPTER 10

JESSE

Jesse means 'king or gift of God.' He lived in Bethlehem, was a wealthy farmer with many sheep, and eight sons. He is the father of David, who killed Goliath and became King of Israel. When God chose a king for the nation of Israel, He sent His prophet Samuel to Jesse's house. Samuel told Jesse to bring his sons outside, because God was going to anoint one of them, as King of Israel.

Jesse had his older seven sons come out, but when Samuel held the horn of oil over their heads, the oil did not pour out. Then, Samuel asked Jesse if he was sure these were all of his sons? Jesse replied that his youngest son was out watching the sheep, and he was too little to be anointed. But Samuel insisted that Jesse bring his youngest son.

Surely enough, when David showed up, and Samuel held the horn of oil over his head, immediately the oil began to pour out, and David was anointed King of Israel.

Where is this story found in the Bible: 1 Samuel 16

Do you remember how many son's Jesse had?

Which one was anointed king of Israel?

CHAPTER 11

KING

King means, one who is given authority, and who has the ability to lead others. It can also mean, ruler over a group or nation of people. There were kings in the old testament and the new testament.

A king generally was to be an anointed representative of God. The nation was blessed as long as the king obeyed God, but destruction and captivity came when the king refused to listen to God, or His prophets.

Some of the king's responsibilities included making many decisions, for all the people in the entire nation, on laws, punishments, arguments etc. He should be honest, fair, and compassionate toward the people he rules over. However, there were many kings who were known to be hateful and ruthless, toward their people. Other responsibilities of a king, were to build up and command the army that would protect him, and the kingdom.

There are two books in the bible, called 1 Kings and 2 Kings, and they give the history of all the kings of Israel and Judah, in the old testament. The most known kings are: King Saul, King David, King Solomon, and the King of Kings - King Jesus!

Where is this story found in the Bible: 1 Kings & 2 Kings

What were some of the responsibilities of a king?

What is the definition of "king?"

CHAPTER 12

LUKE

Luke, a Gentile (meaning he was not from the nation of Israel), is the writer of two books of the bible found in the new testament: The Gospel of Luke and the Book of Acts. He wasn't a disciple, nor did he follow Jesus' ministry firsthand, but he studied documents, and listened to what others said, who had firsthand information about Jesus; one of them was Paul.

His training was that of a physician (doctor) and he used medical terms in some of his writings to describe the sick. However, he is also called one of the Four Evangelists, because his writing tells the 'good news,' known as 'the gospel' of Jesus Christ. He wrote more of the new testament than any other author of the bible.

The "good news," is God's people telling others about salvation and the ministry of Jesus the Christ.

Where is this story found in the Bible: Luke & Acts

What is the Gospel also known as?

What two books did Luke write?

CHAPTER 13

MOSES

Moses means 'to pull out or to draw out.' The story of Moses tells about him being placed in the Nile River, in a basket, by his mother (a Hebrew/Israelite), who was trying to save his life from the soldiers of Pharaoh. He was pulled out or drawn out, of the river by Pharaoh's daughter, who raised the infant in the palace, as an adopted son of the King of Egypt.

Moses was trained to fight with the best soldiers in Egypt and could have possibly been appointed to the throne one day. However, as a man, he began to empathize with his people, and one day witnessed an Egyptian beating a Hebrew slave. Moses came to the rescue of the Hebrew and killed the Egyptian.

Now, the law in Egypt was that anyone who killed an Egyptian, would be put to death. So, when Moses' secret was discovered, he ran for his life and left Egypt. Many years later, God brings him back to Egypt to stand before Pharaoh, and free the Hebrew people.

Moses was most known, as the man who had an encounter with God at the burning bush, and for being chosen to bring redemption to his people, by telling Pharaoh that God said, "Let My People Go!"

God's chosen people had been made slaves in Egypt and had prayed to God for freedom. Moses was the redeemer. Pharaoh was stubborn and refused to release the Hebrews, and ten plagues of God's judgment were brought on the people of Egypt, including the death of all the first-born males in the land, which included the death of Pharaoh's son.

Moses is also well known for being the one to lead the Hebrew people (Israelites) across the Red Sea. Once they left Egypt, they headed toward the sea. God worked one of the most well-known miracles, by parting the waters of the sea and allowing the Hebrews to pass to the other side, on dry land, while drowning Pharaoh's army, who tried to cross behind the Israelites, to kill them.

God also gave Moses the Ten Commandments, which were instructions on how God wanted His people to live, now that they were no longer slaves.

Where is this story found in the Bible: Exodus 2; Exodus 3; Exodus 14

Can you name 5 things Moses did for God's people?

What did Moses tell pharaoh, that God said?

CHAPTER 14

NOAH

Noah means 'rest and peace.' At the time of Noah, people on earth were very corrupt/evil. Violence was all around, and God saw the terrible state that man was in. There was only one person that found favor in the eyes of the Lord, and that was Noah.

So, the Lord told Noah to build an ark, which is a big/huge boat. God also told Noah that He was going to flood the whole earth with water, because of the wickedness of the people. The Lord told Noah that He would spare him and his family's lives, from the flood. Then God gave Noah instructions on how to build the ark.

The Lord also told him to take two of every kind of animal and bird, a male and a female, onto the ark. After Naoh finished building the ark, and got his family and the animals loaded, the flood came and destroyed all of the people on earth. It rained for 40 days and 40 nights. Before the flood, Noah spent years warning his friends and neighbors of what God was about to do, but no one listened.

Where is this story found in the Bible: (Genesis, chapters 5-10)

What did Noah build?

How long did it rain?

CHAPTER 15

ORPAH

Orpah means 'double-minded' or it could mean 'stubborn.' Orpah was a Moabite woman who married one of the sons of Naomi and Elimelech, who were from Bethlehem. First the father, Elimelech died, followed by his two sons. Now that Orpah was a widow and her mother-in-law too, Naomi, was returning back to Bethlehem. Orpah and her sister Ruth, were both encouraged to return to their homes, back to their parents. Naomi had nothing left to offer them. She didn't have money and had lost her husband and two sons.

Both young ladies, Ruth and Orpah, had to decide whether they would go back to their parents in Moab, or stay with Naomi and move to Bethlehem. To stay with Naomi meant to worship the God of Israel, and turn away from idol gods. Orpah made the decision to return to Moab; back to her family.

Where is this story found in the Bible: Ruth 1

Do you think Orpah made a wise choice?

Would it have been better for her to go with Naomi and Ruth, to serve the God of Israel?

CHAPTER 16

PAUL

Paul's name was changed after he came to know Jesus (Acts 9). His name at birth was Saul, which means 'ask/question.' Paul was born a Hebrew of the Benjamite tribe or family. His parents were Pharisees (well-educated and wealthy). Even though they were citizens of Rome, they worshipped in Jerusalem as the sacred, Holy City. Saul became a persecutor of Christians, because he felt that Christianity challenged the traditional laws of the church. Therefore, he set out to persecute all Christians, and either have them put to death, or put in prison. In all of this, he believed he was pleasing God, but he was not. However, one day, as Saul was going on another journey to kill more Christians, he met Jesus. All of a sudden, Saul was blinded by an amazing, bright light and heard his name being called, twice. He answered the Lord, and Jesus asked him, why was he persecuting the church? Saul asked, who was he speaking with, and Jesus said, "I am Jesus, the one you are persecuting." Saul gave his life to Christ at that moment. Jesus gave him instructions to follow afterwards, but when Saul stood up, he was blind. The men with him had to take him to the city Jesus had instructed Saul to go to, and begin preparing for his great ministry, to preach about Jesus. His name was changed to Paul, and he became one of the greatest apostles. He preached the gospel with strong boldness and won many to Christ. He even wrote seven books of the bible: Romans, 1st & 2nd Corinthians, Galatians, Ephesians, Philippians, and Colossians.

Where is this story found in the Bible: Acts 9

Is it possible to think you are right, even when you are wrong?

When did Saul stop killing Christians and putting them in jail?

CHAPTER 17

QUARTUS AND RUTH

Quartus means 'fourth,' and was a name given to the fourth child. He was a Christian in the city of Corinth and led many people to be converted into Christianity. He is mentioned, by Paul, in the book of Romans where he sent greetings to his fellow Christians, in the city of Tarsus.

The scripture refers to him as, 'the brother' and some say he was one of the seventy disciples sent out by Jesus, on a special mission. We still refer to Christians, members of the body of Christ, as sisters and brothers.

Where is this story found in the Bible: Romans 16:23

Have you ever wondered why Christians call themselves brother and sister?

What did Quartus do in Corinth?

Q U A R T U S

RUTH

Ruth is one of the books in the bible named after a woman. She is from Moab and is the daughter-in-law of Naomi. When her husband died, Ruth made a decision to stay with Naomi. Even though Naomi tried to get Ruth to return back to her family, Ruth refused. She made a vow, a commitment, a promise to Naomi that wherever Naomi went, she would go, and Naomi's God would also be her God. Ruth truly loved her mother-in-law and had learned so much about worshipping the true and living God, from her.

Now, because Naomi had lost her husband and both of her sons, she decided to return to her native country in Bethlehem. Ruth went with her. When they reached Bethlehem, Ruth knew she would have to work for food.

Naomi was too old to work in the fields. So, Naomi instructed Ruth on how to work the fields and not cause any trouble, especially since she was from a foreign country. The field that Ruth worked in was owned by Naomi's cousin who was godly, and extremely wealthy.

One day the owner of the field, Boaz, paid attention to her in the fields. He saw how humbled she was and how hard she worked. He told his workers to leave some extra grain in the area where she would be gleaning or gathering grain, so she could bring home more food.

Boaz began to inquire more about Ruth, to find out who was her family. He found out that Naomi was the widow to his kindred, Elimelech.

Later, Boaz followed the Jewish law and married Ruth, who went from rags to riches. They became the great-grandparents of King David.

Where is this story found in the Bible: The Book of Ruth

What shows that Ruth was a woman of loyal character?

Why does the story say Ruth went from rags to riches?

CHAPTER 18

SOLOMON

Solomon, also known as King Solomon, was the son of King David. Before Israel was divided into two nations, there were three kings: King Saul, King David, and King Solomon. Even though he wasn't the only son of King David, he was the only son to be anointed King over all of Israel.

Now, Solomon is most famous for being the wisest and richest man in the world, at that time. Solomon became king after his father David, died and he was still a young boy, around the age of 12. The bible says that GOD spoke to Solomon in a dream and asked him to make a request of anything he wanted. Solomon wanted wisdom to judge the people of Israel wisely, because he was just a boy.

Because Solomon's request was so unselfish, GOD was very pleased, and not only did He give Solomon wisdom, but also great riches, long-life, and peace, with all nations surrounding Israel. Kings and queens from all around, admired Solomon's wisdom and riches, because he was far richer than all the kings or queens known in the earth.

Now, Solomon wasn't just wise in ruling the people. He was also wise in engineering, and created the detailed plans for constructing amazing buildings, gardens, roads, as well as a fleet of ships. His greatest building project was the Jewish Temple, where the Israelites would come to worship GOD and bring their offerings.

Even though GOD warned Solomon not to marry wives that didn't worship HIM, the one and only true God, Solomon had 700 wives and 300 concubines (like a girlfriend or someone having a lower status than a wife), many of them were foreign women, who worshipped idol gods.

Over the years, Solomon's heart began to fall away from GOD, and he started worshipping idol gods, with his wives.

He even built small temples, called high places, where the idol gods could be worshipped. Eventually, the Lord became angry with Solomon for not following HIS commands, and Solomon was punished.

Solomon wrote three books of the bible: The Song of Solomon, Ecclesiastes, and much of the book of Proverbs.

<u>Where is this story found in the Bible: 1 Kings</u>

How old was Solomon, when he became king?

Do you think it is a bad idea to not listen to God's instructions?

CHAPTER 19

TIMOTHY

Timothy, also known as Timotheus, was born around A.D. 17. He was the son of a Jewish mother, whose name was Eunice, who was a believer of God, and the son of a Greek father. His grandmother, on his mother's side, was named Lois, and she was a believer of God too.

His father left Timothy in the hands of his mother and grandmother. He was taught by them, about scriptures, when he was a child. Timothy was in his early 20s or 30s when he met Paul. He was an unmarried man. He was a very faithful servant of God at a church. He was a Pastor. Paul said Timothy was an apostle, meaning a messenger, he who is sent by God, to deliver and spread the word of God. Timothy was highly recommended by several church members to accompany Paul as he traveled, preaching the gospel, while also convincing the Jews, that Jesus was the Messiah. Timothy was ordained to serve by Paul and a church brother. Timothy was dedicated to spreading the gospel.

Paul was in prison in Rome, when he requested his friend Timothy to come see him. Paul wrote two letters to Timothy instructing him in the ways of church leadership; those letters are 1 and 2 Timothy.

<u>Where is this story found in the Bible: Acts 16; 1 & 2 Timothy</u>

What was Timothy's other name?

When was Timothy first taught about scriptures?

CHAPTER 20

UZZIAH

The Hebrew name **Uzziah** means, 'Yah is my strength.' Uzziah was also known by the name, Azariah. Uzziah was the tenth King of Judah, as well as one of the sons of Amaziah. He was 16 years old when he became King of Judah, and reigned for 52 years. He and his father were co-rulers of Judah, until his father died. After his father's death, Uzziah became the sole ruler of Judah. Uzziah was faithful to God and he did what was right, in the eyes of the Lord. He was influenced by Zachariah, the prophet. He made machines to use on the building of towers, and on the corner defenses, for shooting arrows and hurling large stones. He conquered the Philistines and the Arabians and received tribute from the Ammonites. He organized and re-equipped the army. He refortified the country, and was a vigorous and able ruler. His name spread abroad, even to the entrance of Egypt. He became very popular. Then his pride took over, and this is what led to his downfall.

One day, he went into the temple to burn incense. Only the priests were allowed to do this. Therefore, he was struck with leprosy, for disobeying God, at which time his son Jotham took over the government. While Uzziah was still alive, he had to live in another house until he died.

Where is this story found in the Bible: 2 Chronicles

What did God do to Uzziah?

Why?

CHAPTER 21

VICTORY

Victory means to win. Thanks be to God, because it is God who gives us the victory. We get victory when God fights our battles for us. Victory was given to us when Jesus died on the cross.

We get victory when we are healed by the precious blood of Jesus. Victory can be achieved, when we have faith, and place our trust in God.

When the Egyptians were drowned in the Red Sea, it was celebrated as a victory, because God's people were safe from harm.

When we are healed, we claim the victory. It is said, many times, that the Lord gives us victory through our enemies, because He protects us from our enemies.

Where is this story found in the Bible: 1 John 5:4; Deuteronomy 20:4

How can one attain victory?

Name one way you can claim victory in your life?

CHAPTER 22

WORLD

World refers to the earth and the universe. God created this world. He is the creator of all things! In this world there are believers of our Lord and Savior Jesus Christ, who are physically present in the world, but not of the world. This means, we can be here in this world, but we do not have to do the bad or wrong things, some people do.

As believers, we are to be set apart from a world of sin and wickedness. Those types of people of the world, live in darkness. They do not live a holy and righteous life.

To be set apart, means you change the behavior of your old self, and be transformed into a new person, which is not easily done on our own.

We have to want to be more Christ like, trust God, and have faith so that we can be transformed, by the renewing of our minds. That means, by thinking and behaving in a way, that is pleasing to God.

We want to be light to those in darkness. That light should shine in us everywhere we go, so others can see there is something different about us.

Where is this story found in the Bible: Genesis 1

What makes someone a worldly person?

Is it easy for a person to change? How?

CHAPTER 23

XERXES

XERXES, also known as Ahasuerus, the King of Persia, plays a prominent role in the book of Esther. He was the son of King Darius, and he was also a very powerful ruler of the Persian empire.

During the third year of Xerxes' reign, he held a huge feast unto all of his princes and servants, to show off all of his wealth and riches, to the governors and officials of his empire.

He also had a wife named, Queen Vashti. During that same time frame, the Queen was holding a celebration for the women of the empire.

After seven days of eating and drinking, King Xerxes asked for his wife Queen Vashti, to come into the banquet where he was, so that he could show off her beauty, to those who were in attendance, but she refused to go.

This made the King very angry. Because of her disobedience to her husband, King Xerxes, she was asked to never come before the King again. He also sent out word, to the people, that women were not to follow Queen Vashti's regrettable example of not obeying their husbands.

The king sent out word for all beautiful, pure women to gather into the King's harem, so the king could choose himself, a new Queen.

A Jewish woman named Esther, who was raised by her cousin Mordecai, after her parents died, was one of the women rounded up for King Xerxes. Esther was an extremely beautiful woman. She was eventually selected to become the new queen, because she won the heart of the king, but she kept her nationality as a Jew a secret, as Mordecai asked her to do.

They honored her presence, and she requested a two-day banquet with the King and the Prime Minister Haman. God used Queen Esther and her cousin, who was now Prime Minister Mordecai, to save the Jewish people from being exterminated, while under the rule of Prime Minister Haman.

The Festival of Purim, was established by Mordecai to remind the Jewish people how they were saved, by Queen Esther and Mordecai, from extermination.

Where is this story found in the Bible: The Book of Esther

Why was Esther important in this story?

The Festival of Purim was established for what reason?

CHAPTER 24

YAHWEH

Yahweh, is a personal name of God. God has no shortage of names. He is called by over 1000 names, but one of these names stands alone, and that name is Yahweh.

In some English language Bibles, it is written in all capital letters as "LORD." His name was revealed to Moses as four Hebrew consonants, with no vowels: YHWH, also known as the tetragrammaton. The name Jehovah, is most widely used, and is also translated as 'The Lord'.

Yahweh, is a form of the Hebrew name of God used in the Bible. Jews did not use the name Yahweh, because the name was respected as too sacred for people to speak.

The meaning of the name has been interpreted to mean "He Who Makes That Which Has Been Made," or "He Brings Into Existence Whatever Exists."

Where is this story found in the Bible: Exodus 6:3; Exodus 17:15; Psalm 83:18

Do you know some other names that God is called?

When you pray, what name do you call Him?

CHAPTER 25

ZADOK

Zadok means, 'just' or 'righteous'. He was the son of Ahitub, and a Levite priest, during the time of David. For a long time, he was co-high priest, with Abiathar.

He was a descendent of Aaron, and also a leader over his family of Levite's.

There are several other men named Zadok, in the Bible, but they are only mentioned in one or two versus each. There is Zadok the descendent of Zadok the priest, Zadok the Levite, Zadok the father of Jerusha, Zadok the son of Baana, Zadok the son of Immer, Zadok the Israelite leader, Zadok the scribe, and Zadok, an ancestor of Jesus Christ.

Where is this story found in the Bible: 2 Samuel; 1 Kings; 1 Chronicles

What about Zadok, makes you think he knew something about God?

What does the name, Zadok mean?

BIBLICAL STORIES FROM A-Z

ANOTHER BOOK BY TARSHA PHILLIPS

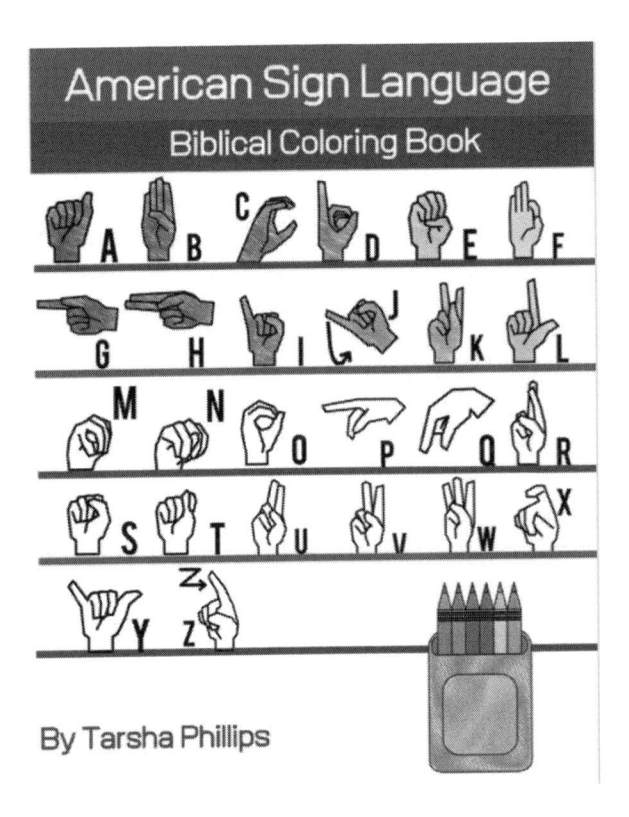

American Sign Language Biblical Coloring Book

By Tarsha Phillips

BIBLICAL STORIES FROM A-Z

Made in the USA
Columbia, SC
10 February 2023